D0131074

SUPER
More
Friendship Crafts

Written and illustrated by
Charlene Olexiewicz

LOWELL HOUSE JUVENILE

LOS ANGELES

NTC/Contemporary Publishing Group

To Nami, my lifelong best friend.
—C. O.

NOTE: The numbered pinwheel in the upper right corner of each project indicates the level of difficulty—1 being the easiest and 3 the hardest.

Published by Lowell House
A division of NTC/Contemporary Publishing Group, Inc.
4255 West Touhy Avenue, Lincolnwood (Chicago), Illinois 60712 U.S.A.

Managing Director and Publisher: Jack Artenstein
Director of Publishing Services: Rena Copperman
Editorial Director: Brenda Pope-Ostrow
Director of Art Production: Bret Perry
Project Editor: Amy Downing
Editorial Assistant: Jacqueline Jabourian
Designer: Carolyn Wendt
Cover Photos: Ann Bogart

Lowell House books can be purchased at special discounts
when ordered in bulk for premiums and special sales.
Contact Customer Service at the address above,
or call 1-800-323-4900.

Printed and bound in the United States of America

Library of Congress Catalog Card Number: 00-131156

ISBN: 0-7373-0501-0

RCP 10 9 8 7 6 5 4 3 2 1

Contents

Bud O'Mine

Make a bud for your bud! This chocolate rosebud is a sweet way to show you care.

What You'll Need

- clear tape
- two wrapped chocolate candies (such as Hershey's Kisses)
- 6-inch square of pink or red cellophane
- scissors
- ruler
- green tissue paper
- 18-gauge wire, 9 inches long
- green floral tape
- satin ribbon (optional)

Directions

1. Take a short length of tape and loop it around on itself. Use this loop of tape to secure the two chocolates together, bottom to bottom.

2. Place the pointed tip of one of the chocolates in the center of the 6-inch square of cellophane. Gather up the edges of the cellophane and twist the cellophane tight around the chocolates. Wrap a piece of tape around the twisted cellophane. Use scissors to trim off the excess cellophane below the tape.

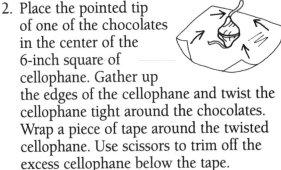

3. Cut a 2-inch square from the green tissue paper. Cut out the four triangle shapes as indicated by the dashed lines in the illustration. You should now have a four-pointed star shape.

4. Fold the star shape in half and cut a small slit into the folded edge. Unfold the star shape and slip the bottom of the bud through the slit, pushing the tissue paper all the way up to the base of the bud.

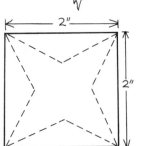

5. Poke the wire up into the bottom of the bud. Wrap the base of the bud with a little tape to secure the tissue paper and wire.

4

6. Begin at the base of the bud and start wrapping the stem with floral tape. Remember to slightly stretch the floral tape as you wrap in a downward angle. (Floral tape gets tacky when it is stretched, which makes it stick to the wire.) Stop wrapping when the floral tape is about 1 or 2 inches below the base of the bud.

7. Cut a double leaf shape from the green tissue paper by following the diagram shown here. Twist the double leaf shape at the center a couple of rotations. Hold the twisted center of the leaves on the stem just below the floral tape. Continue wrapping the floral tape around the stem, trapping the leaves as you go. Finish wrapping the stem and cut off the excess tape at the bottom. For that extra-sweet friend, make three or more rosebuds and tie them together with a pretty satin ribbon.

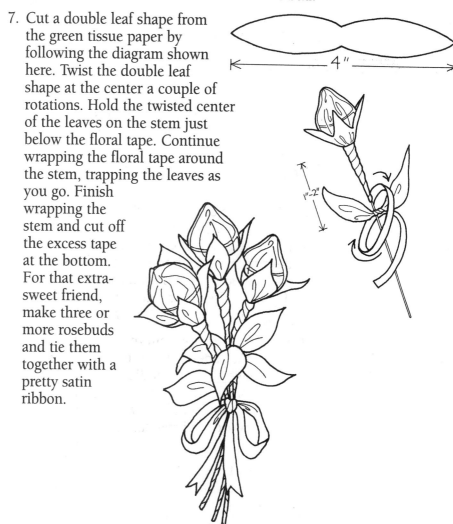

One Step Further

Glue a piece of Styrofoam to the inside of a small 2- to 3-inch clay pot. Stick three or more rosebuds into the Styrofoam. Place peat moss into the pot to hide the Styrofoam. What a sweet arrangement.

Guardian Angel

Make this guardian angel for your friend's bedroom door. She will stand watch over your pal and keep her safe.

- scissors
- two paper plates
- ruler
- glue
- color pencils or markers
- three or four cotton balls
- masking tape
- two craft feathers, any color
- metallic gold pipe cleaner

Directions

1. Cut one paper plate into a triangular shape as shown. Cut a 3-inch circle out of the center of another paper plate. Glue the circle onto the point of the triangle.

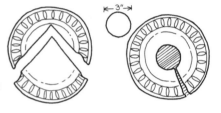

2. Use color pencils or markers to draw the face of the angel. Follow the illustration to draw the arms and hands. Sketch a rectangular sign for the angel to hold in her hands that reads "[your friend's name] Room." You can color the angel's gown with patterns and designs.

3. Pour glue along the top edge of the head. Shred up three or four cotton balls for hair and glue the pieces on. Allow the glue to dry.

4. Turn the angel over. Use masking tape to attach two craft feathers onto the back side for wings.

5. Measure 3 inches up from the end of the pipe cleaner and bend it at a right angle. Loop the pipe cleaner around to make a halo, then twist it closed. Cut off any excess. Tape the halo to the back side of the head with masking tape. Your friend can attach her new angel to her door with masking tape.

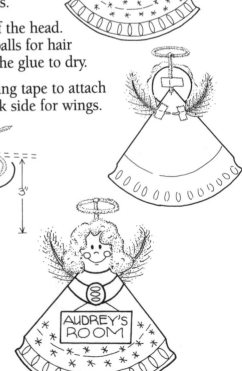

Sublime Slime

You and your friends will have fun making this batch of slime. Divvy it up, and get ready for a sublime slime time! It's great to give away as party favors, too!

What You'll Need

- two bowls
- two plastic spoons
- 2 cups white glue
- 1½ cups water
- food coloring, any color
- ⅓ cup warm water
- 1 tablespoon 20 Mule Team Borax
- six sandwich-size plastic bags
- curling ribbon

Directions

1. In one bowl, use a plastic spoon to mix together the glue and the water. Add two or three drops of food coloring and mix completely.

2. In the second bowl, use another spoon to mix the ⅓ cup warm water and Borax.

3. Add the Borax mixture to the glue mixture in the first bowl. The slime will quickly clump.

4. Grab the clump with your hands (ewww!) and squeeze out the excess water.

5. Divide the clump into six equal pieces. Put each piece into a sandwich-size plastic bag and tie each closed with a piece of curling ribbon. Be sure to squeeze as much air as possible out of the bags when you package the slime. The slime will stay fresh as long as the bag is airtight. Wash both bowls in warm, soapy water and rinse well.

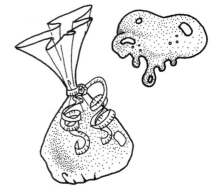

Wheel of Fortune

ADULT SUPERVISION RECOMMENDED
You and your friends will have great laughs and fun playing with this wheel of fortune.

What You'll Need

- 6- to 8-inch round bowl
- lightweight white cardboard or poster board, at least a 10-inch square
- pencil
- scissors
- ruler
- markers, eight different colors
- black fine-tip marker
- hole punch
- pushpin
- brass fastener

Directions

1. Place the bowl upside down on the cardboard or poster board. Use the pencil to trace around the outside of the bowl. Cut out the circle you just made.

2. Use the ruler and pencil to divide the circle into eight equal pie shapes.

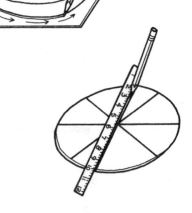

3. Using markers, color in each pie shape a different color. Use the black fine-tip marker and ruler to darken the lines between the pie shapes.

4. With the black marker, write eight possible answers to a yes or no question in each pie shape. Here are some suggestions: "Absolutely Yes!"; "No Way!"; "Not Sure"; "Ask Again"; "Maybe"; and so on. Draw question marks to fill any empty spaces on the wheel.

5. It's time to make the spinner. Use the illustration shown here as a guide. Draw the spinner on the leftover cardboard and cut it out. Use the hole punch to put a hole in the rounded end of the spinner. (Be sure not to put the hole too close to the edges.) Use a marker to color in the spinner.

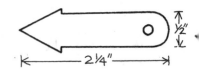

6. Have an adult use the pushpin to poke a hole in the center of the wheel. Attach the spinner to the wheel using a brass fastener. Twist the fastener around and around until the hole becomes big enough for the fastener to rotate freely. Separate the two pieces of the fastener on the back side of the wheel, but don't make it too tight.

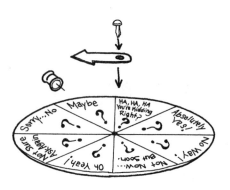

7. The wheel is ready, so ask away! Ask a yes or no question, then spin the wheel. It will give you an answer. If the pointer lands on a line, spin again.

5

Bunny Buddy

This cute little bunny makes a great gift or party favor.

What You'll Need

- baby washcloth, any color (regular washcloths are too thick)
- rubber band
- ruler
- thread
- needle
- two tiny black seed beads
- white pom-pom, ¾-inch size
- scissors
- ¼-inch-wide satin ribbon, 10 inches long

Directions

1. Place the washcloth in a diamond shape with the bumpier side facedown. Starting at the top point, tightly roll it downward until you reach the center. Tightly roll the bottom point up to the center.

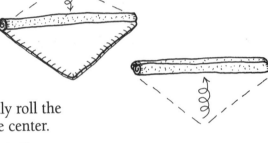

2. Bend the washcloth in half, making sure the two rolls are on the inside and the outside is seamless. Position the washcloth as shown in the illustration.

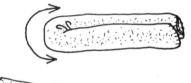

3. Bend the washcloth in half by bringing over the right end to meet the left end.

4. Tie a rubber band around the washcloth approximately 1 inch in from the right end to create the head.

5. Pull the ears up. Sew on the beads for the eyes and the pom-pom for the tail. Tie the ribbon around the neck into a little bow to finish off your bunny. That was so easy, you'll want to make another!

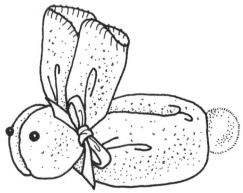

10

H₂0 Glow Light

To add a little enchantment to your next slumber party, have each of your guests make one of these night-lights. They'll make the whole room glow!

What You'll Need

- plastic water bottle, 24- to 32-ounce size
- water
- variety of found items small enough to fit through the neck of the bottle (such as plastic figurines, plastic play jewelry, small rubber balls, marbles, plastic charms, beads, pearls, seashells, and plastic buttons)
- glow-in-the-dark plastic stars
- sequins, rhinestones, and glitter
- glow stick (the kind used at Halloween and the Fourth of July)

Directions

1. Soak the water bottle in warm, soapy water for a few minutes and then remove the label. Rinse the bottle to remove any excess soap.

2. Add water to the bottle until it is about three-quarters full.

3. Drop all your found items into the water bottle. Add some sequins, rhinestones, glitter, and glow-in-the-dark stars. (The stars will bend a little to fit through the neck of the bottle.)

4. Fill the bottle the rest of the way with water. Just before "slumber-time," activate the glow stick and put it in your water bottle. (Most brands of glow sticks come with a cap that has a loop on it. That cap should pull off easily, leaving you with a plain glow tube.) To activate the glow stick, bend it until you hear it snap and then give it a little shake. The glow stick should glow brightly for 12 to 24 hours. After the glow stick is in the bottle, put the top back onto the water bottle tightly, then party on!

7 Media Mania

Do you and your friends like to listen to music, watch TV, and go to the movies together? Well, this journal will be a fun way to log the "media moments" you've spent together.

What You'll Need

- old magazines and weekly TV listings
- scissors
- composition book (available where student supplies are sold)
- white glue
- paper plate
- paintbrush
- construction paper
- colorful markers
- ticket stubs, receipts, and programs from concerts, movies, and plays that you've been to

Directions

1. Look through some old magazines and TV listings, and cut out anything that has to do with music, TV, theater, or the movies. You can cut out pictures of your favorite singers or movie and TV stars. Cut out key words such as "movie," "Hollywood," "diva," "music," and "TV." Try to find your name, too!

2. Arrange the cutouts on the cover of the composition book in a collage style. Keep moving the elements around until you are pleased with the design. Overlap and angle the cutouts for a completed collage effect.

3. Remove the cutouts from the book and carefully place them in the same pattern on the table next to the book.

4. Pour out some white glue onto the paper plate. Use a paintbrush to spread the glue over the upper third of the book cover. Place the cutouts onto the book. Cover the next third with glue and add the cutouts. Finally, do the same with the lower third.

5. The collage cover needs a finishing coat to completely seal the cutouts. Use the paintbrush to apply a layer of white glue over the entire cover. Don't panic if the finished coat looks milky at first. It will dry clear. Clean the brush with warm, soapy water and rinse well. Allow the cover to dry overnight before going on to the next step.

6. Open up the book. Cut a piece of construction paper to fit the lower half of the inside cover. Squirt a line of glue along the two sides and bottom of the paper and place it on the inside cover. You have just created a pocket to hold programs. Cut another piece of construction paper that is half the size of the first.  Glue it in the same way along the bottom edge of the book. This shallow pocket will hold ticket stubs and receipts. (Repeat this step on the back cover if you want another set of pockets.)

7. Use colorful markers to write "Programs" and "Tickets & Receipts" on the pockets.

8. When you and your friends go to the movies, the theater, or a concert, or watch TV together, make an entry in your new media journal. Write down the show's title and date, and who you saw it with. Write your thoughts on the event and performers, including what you liked or disliked about it. Would  you recommend others to see it and why or why not? You can even give the event a star rating, with four stars for a terrific show and one star for a real stinker!

Light Up Her Life

This candleholder is the perfect friendship gift. When the candle is burning, your friend will enjoy its colorful glow.

What You'll Need

- clear glass candleholder, votive size
- scissors
- tissue paper, variety of pastel colors
- ruler
- newspaper
- white glue
- paper plate
- small brush
- votive candle (white would look best)

Directions

1. Before you begin, you'll have to give a little thought as to what design you want on the candleholder. You can do tulips, stars, polka dots, rainbows, butterflies, checkerboard, hearts, or whatever you wish. If you want to keep it simple, you can do an abstract pattern of overlapping torn tissue pieces. It's up to you!

2. If you decide to cut out patterns (such as tulips, butterflies, or hearts), you'll need to use scissors and cut those shapes out of tissue paper first. Set them aside.

3. Tear some tissue paper into small irregular shapes. (The shapes should measure no bigger than ¾ inch in any one direction.) Tear up enough pieces to cover the outside of the holder.

4. Cover your work surface with newspaper. Pour a quarter-size puddle of white glue onto a paper plate. Dip the brush into the glue and apply it to the outside of the holder. Don't try to cover a large area. A 1-inch-square section at a time is big enough.

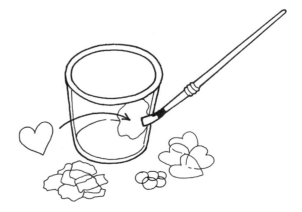

5. If your design includes cutout shapes such as tulips, hearts, and so on, you'll need to glue them on first. After each shape is put down, brush a little glue over the top of it to fully seal it.

6. Continue to brush on glue and add the small torn pieces to fill the spaces in between. Don't be afraid to overlap the tissue pieces over each other and over the cutout shapes. Be sure to brush a little glue over the top of each piece as you go.

7. Once the entire outside of the holder is covered with tissue paper, allow it to dry overnight. The white glue will dry clear. Clean the brush out with warm, soapy water and rinse well. Add a white votive candle to the holder and give it to a special friend.

Note: Always get an adult to light a candle, and never leave a burning candle unattended.

Friendship Pin

Give a cherished friend this special pin made just for her.

What You'll Need

- graph paper
- pencil
- tiny glass (or seed) beads, assorted colors
- 10 small safety pins, ⅞ inch long
- one large safety pin, 1½ inches long

Directions

1. You'll need to make a layout of your design on graph paper first. Draw a rectangle on the graph paper that is 10 squares wide and 8 squares high. Each square represents a bead.

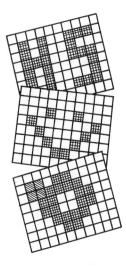

2. Decide what design you want to do, such as a smiley face, flower, or heart, or just simple stripes of color. Darken in one square at a time to lay out your design. You can even do your friend's initials.

3. Choose two colors of beads that your friend will like. Be sure that one color is light and one dark.

4. Use your layout as a guide to load the beads onto the 10 small safety pins. Each vertical row of eight squares you see on your layout represents one safety pin. For example, look at the sample layout of the heart shown here. If you choose to do this heart design, you'd start with the far left row of the vertical squares. Open up one small safety pin and load it with eight light-colored beads. Close the pin.

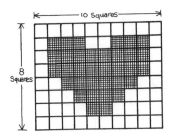

5. Open up the large safety pin and slip the smaller pin onto it.

6. Look at the next vertical row on the heart layout. Load the second small safety pin with one light-colored bead, three dark-colored beads, and four light-colored beads. Close the pin and slip it onto the larger one.

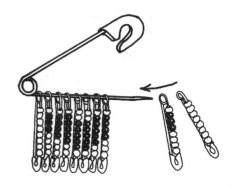

7. Using your layout as a guide, continue loading the pins and placing them onto the large pin until you are done. Close the large pin. If you want, you can make another matching pin for yourself.

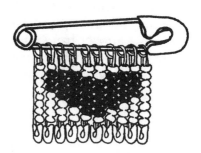

Play Ball!

You and your friends will enjoy playing with these bouncing balls, each one complete with a colorful tail.

What You'll Need

- multicolored rubber bands, assorted sizes (1½-ounce package)
- scissors
- ruler
- regular and/or metallic curling ribbon, any color

Directions

1. Your package of rubber bands should contain about 150 rubber bands. You'll need about 50 rubber bands per ball, so you'll be able to make three balls. Start with a medium-size rubber band and knot it three or four times.

2. Take a second rubber band (of any size) and wrap and twist it around the knotted one. It is helpful to twist the rubber band two or three rotations between each wrap. Continue to wrap and twist the rubber band until it is used up and tightly secured.

3. Continue adding rubber bands. As you do so, try to evenly distribute the rubber bands to avoid making a lopsided ball. It is a bit awkward to handle the ball when it is small, but be patient. Once the ball gets bigger, it becomes easier to handle.

4. Stop when you've used up about 50 rubber bands. The ball should be the size of a walnut. Cut three 28-inch lengths of curling ribbon. Gather the three ribbons together, making sure the ends match up. Slip a rubber band onto the ribbons at their halfway point. Fold the ribbons in half and knot them together at the rubber band.

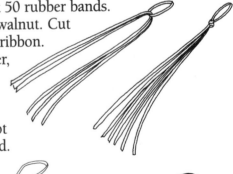

5. Wrap and twist the rubber band with the ribbons attached onto the ball. That's it!

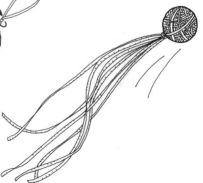

Hair Jewels

You and your gal pal can do each other's hair, then adorn the do's with these sparkling jewels.

What You'll Need

- Velcro (black if you have dark-colored hair, white if you have light or blonde hair)
- scissors
- small rhinestones, any color
- tacky craft glue

Directions

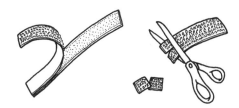

1. Separate the Velcro pieces. For this craft, you're going to use only the rough piece of Velcro, the side with the tiny loops on it. (You will not need the smooth, soft piece.) Cut tiny pieces of rough Velcro to fit the backs of the rhinestone jewels.

2. Using tacky craft glue, glue a Velcro piece onto the back of each rhinestone. Allow the glue to dry. That's it!

3. Get together with a friend who likes to do hair. Experiment with different looks—half up/half down, braids, ponytails, buns, and so on. Simply place the jewels onto the hair wherever you want them. They will stick!

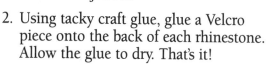

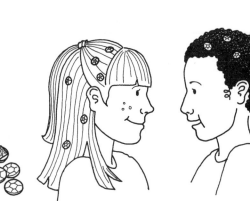

One Step Further

You can even make hair charms by gluing Velcro to the back of small metal and plastic charms. You and your friend will look absolutely stunning!

For Keepsake!

Store your friendship treasures in this cute keepsake box.

What You'll Need

- scissors
- ruler
- plastic canvas, at least 10 by 12 inches
- embroidery floss, various colors
- embroidery needle with a large eye
- variety of colorful buttons

Directions

1. Cut six 4-inch squares from the plastic canvas. Be sure that all the edges are smooth and straight.

2. Stack one of the canvas squares on top of another one, making sure to line up the holes.

3. Cut a 16-inch length of embroidery floss (any color). Insert one end of the floss through the bottom left hole of the canvas squares and tie a tight knot.

4. Thread the other end of the floss onto the embroidery needle. You're going to sew the two canvas squares together up the left side. Starting at the bottom, loop the needle into each hole, pulling the floss tight as you go up. When you reach the top hole, tie a tight knot. Trim any excess floss at both the bottom and top.

5. Repeat Steps 2, 3, and 4 using two other canvas squares, but for fun, use a different color floss.

6. It's time to assemble the four sides of the box. Open up the two sets of squares so that they are at right angles. Bring the two sets together as shown. Now 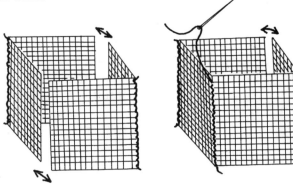 sew the two sets together using the same sewing technique described in Steps 3 and 4. (Remember to use different colors of floss.)

7. Place another canvas square on top of the assembled sides. This will be the bottom of the box. Sew the bottom on along the outer four edges. You can use a different color floss for each of the four edges, or make it all one color.

8. Flip over the box so that it is now resting on its bottom. To decorate the plain top edges, loop embroidery floss around three of them. (Again, use different colors.)

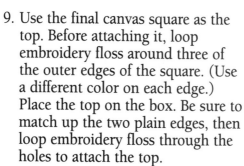

9. Use the final canvas square as the top. Before attaching it, loop embroidery floss around three of the outer edges of the square. (Use a different color on each edge.) Place the top on the box. Be sure to match up the two plain edges, then loop embroidery floss through the holes to attach the top.

10. Sew on a variety of colorful buttons to decorate your keepsake box.

Party Piñata

Your next party will be a real "hit" with this easy-to-make piñata.

What You'll Need

- scissors
- construction paper, various colors
- one medium to large paper shopping bag (with handles)
- glue
- ruler or yardstick
- crepe party streamers, two or three different colors
- variety of candy
- stapler
- cord

Directions

1. Cut pieces of construction paper to fit the outer sides and bottom of the bag. Make it fun and use different colors. Glue them onto the outside of the bag.

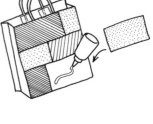

2. Measure the height of the bag and add 24 to 36 inches to that number. Cut about 12 lengths of party streamers to that measurement.

3. Starting at the top left rim of the bag, glue a streamer down the side. The excess streamer will hang freely beyond the bottom of the bag.

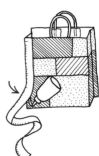

4. Continue gluing on the streamers, leaving a gap about the width of one or two streamers between them. Go all around the bag. (Cut more streamers if you need them.) Allow the glue to dry.

5. Place a variety of your favorite candies in the bag. Staple the top closed in a couple of places and use cord to hang it up as you would any piñata.

One Step Further

Instead of using pieces of construction paper to cover the bag, use pieces of colorful wrapping paper that match the theme of the party.

Stick 'em Up!

ADULT SUPERVISION REQUIRED
Display your friendship memorabilia (photos, cards, artwork, and so on) on this custom-made bulletin board. No tacks or pushpins needed!

What You'll Need

- lightweight cotton fabric, 24 by 28 inches, any color and pattern
- cotton twine, 24 inches long
- heavyweight cardboard or illustration board, 20 by 24 inches
- yardstick or measuring tape
- staple gun (to be used only by an adult)
- small pile of newspapers
- tacky craft glue (or hot glue gun with adult supervision)
- batting, 20 by 24 inches
- masking tape
- scissors
- 6½ yards of ½-inch- or ⅝-inch-wide satin ribbon, any color
- pencil

Directions

1. When you go shopping for supplies, choose a colorful print fabric that will go well in your room. First, you're going to make the hanger for the back side of the bulletin board. Make a large triple knot on each end of the cotton twine. Place one knot down onto the cardboard about 2 inches from the left side and 7 inches down from the top. Have an adult use the staple gun to staple the twine down into the cardboard just to the right of the knot. Do the same on the board's right side with the other knot, this time stapling the twine just to the left of the knot. (Be sure your work surface is protected with a pile of newspapers just in case the staple should poke through to the other side.)

2. Turn the board over. Squirt a line of tacky craft glue all around the outer edges of the board. Place the batting on top. Use a few pieces of masking tape to keep the batting in place so you can keep working while the glue dries.

3. Place the cotton fabric down flat on your work surface with the fabric's printed side facedown. Center the cardboard on top of the upside-down fabric with the batting side facedown.

4. Wrap all four edges of the fabric up over the cardboard and glue them down. Put strips of masking tape along the fabric edges.

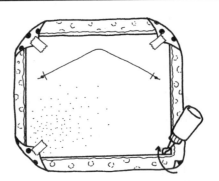

Turn the board over, and make sure that the fabric is tight and there are no creases. If the fabric needs readjusting, do it now before the glue dries.

5. Cut two 36-inch lengths of satin ribbon. Place one ribbon diagonally across the fabric-covered board going from the top left to the bottom right corner. Glue the ends of the ribbons to the back side of the board and use pieces of masking tape to hold them in place. Do the same with the other length of ribbon going from the top right to the bottom left corner.

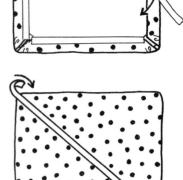

6. Use a yardstick (or measuring tape) and a pencil to make a small mark at the center point of all four edges of the board. Along the top and bottom edges, you will make a small mark at 12 inches. Along the right and left sides, you will make a mark at 10 inches.

7. Cut four 20-inch lengths of satin ribbon. Place one ribbon on the board going from the left side center mark to the bottom edge center mark. Glue the ends of the ribbons to the back side of the board and secure them with masking tape.

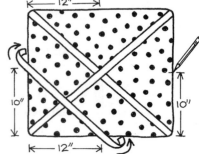

8. Repeat Step 7 with the remaining three lengths of ribbon going from center mark to center mark.

9. Again, protect the work surface with a pile of newspapers. Have an adult use the staple gun to staple the five spots where the ribbons intersect.

10. Cut five 12-inch lengths of satin ribbon. Tie each one into a neat bow and glue them over the staples where the ribbons intersect. (You might want to put a temporary piece of tape over the bows to keep them in place, then remove the tape once the glue is dry.)

Hang your new bulletin board up. To display your memorabilia, simply slip the items under the ribbons. You don't need pins!

15 Friendship Survival Kit

Is your friend down in the dumps? Cheer her up with this survival kit and remind her that she is loved.

What You'll Need

- 32-ounce Chinese food takeout container, 4 inches wide by 3 inches deep by 4 inches high
- scissors
- white and red construction paper
- glue
- red and black pens

- survival kit items: miniature address book, heart-shaped charm, packet of tissues, taffy candy, wax lips, toothpick, and a piece of rock candy
- white notepaper
- hole punch
- red satin ribbon, 14 inches long

Directions

1. You can buy Chinese takeout food containers from a warehouse-type store. Or the next time your family orders Chinese takeout, ask for an extra container. If the container has any writing on it, you'll want to cover it. Cut out two pieces of white construction paper to fit the front and back sides of the box. Glue the construction paper onto the box.

2. Use the graphic design shown here as a guide. Use a red pen to draw a first aid symbol (a circle with a cross in it) on the front of the box. Use a black pen to write the words "Friendship Survival Kit."

3. Gather all the survival kit items, put them in the box, and close it. (Be sure to write your name, address, and phone number in the address book.) If you want to make your own rock candy, follow the recipe on page 45.

4. Cut a piece of white notepaper to measure 3 by 6 inches. Write the following on the piece of paper:

To: _____ From: _____

IN CASE OF EMERGENCY,
OPEN IMMEDIATELY TO REMIND YOU:

Address Book – Call me anytime.
Tissues – If you need a shoulder to cry on, mine is always available.
Toothpick – I'm on your side if you're being picked on.
Taffy Candy – I'm here for you even when things get sticky.
Wax Lips – My lips are sealed if you want to share a secret.
Rock Candy – Our friendship is as solid as rock.
Heart Charm – You are greatly loved.

5. Cut a piece of red construction paper to measure 4 by 7 inches. Glue the survival list centered onto the red paper. Use a hole punch to put a hole at the top. Tie the list onto the handle of the box with a piece of red satin ribbon.

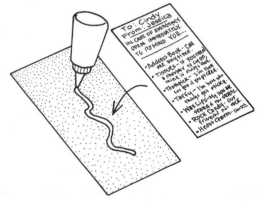

Three-Way Buddy Bracelet

Do you have two best friends who are also best friends? Well, then you have a unique three-way friendship. Get the trio together so that each of you can make one of these bracelets to celebrate your special friendship.

What You'll Need

- felt, three different colors, each 9 by 12 inches
- ruler
- scissors
- clear tape
- embroidery floss, same three colors as the felt

Directions

1. Each of you needs to select your favorite color of felt. (It's best that they be three different colors.) Each color will represent the girl that chose it. The directions that follow explain how to make one bracelet. Each girl will make her own bracelet, so each of you needs to follow every step. When you are done, you should have three identical bracelets.

2. With the help of a ruler for measuring, cut three ¼-by-12-inch strips of felt (one from each color).

3. Stack the strips on top of one another and wrap one end with a piece of tape. Use another piece of tape to secure the felt pieces to your work surface as shown.

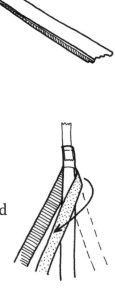

4. It's time to braid the three strips together. Fan out the three pieces, bringing the bottom piece to the left, the center piece to the right, and the top piece straight down in the middle.

5. Lift the right strip up and bring it over toward the left, turning it over as you go. Stop when it comes to rest between the other two strips.

6. Keeping it flat, pull the new right strip further to the right.

7. Lift the left strip up and bring it over toward the right, turning it over as you go. Stop when it comes to rest between the other two strips.

8. The braid pattern has now been started. Continue moving and turning over the right and then the left strips to the middle until the braid is complete. Wrap a piece of tape around the bottom end. You can now remove the piece of tape that has been holding the strips to the work surface.

9. Cut three 12-inch pieces of embroidery floss (one in each color). Gather together all three pieces of floss evenly and tie them tightly around the braid about 1½ inches from the end. (It's important that you tie and knot as tightly as possible.) Trim the excess braid about ¼ to ⅜ inch above the floss.

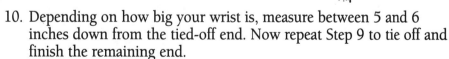

10. Depending on how big your wrist is, measure between 5 and 6 inches down from the tied-off end. Now repeat Step 9 to tie off and finish the remaining end.

11. Help each other tie your bracelets on. (You can use knots or bows.) The three intertwining colors are a symbol of your unbreakable three-way friendship.

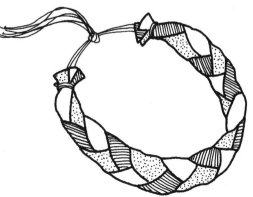

EZ CD Holder

ADULT SUPERVISION REQUIRED
Do you want to be able to find your favorite CDs in a hurry? Get organized with this easy-to-make holder that holds up to 22 CDs.

What You'll Need

- large family-size tissue box (the kind that holds 250 tissues)
- ruler
- sharp pair of scissors
- masking tape
- heavyweight cardboard, 9 by 4 inches
- tacky craft glue
- three pieces black felt, 9 by 12 inches
- two pieces pink felt, 9 by 12 inches

Directions

1. Lay the tissue box on its side. Have an adult score a line that is ½ inch up from the bottom edge. To score the line, have the adult open up the scissors and run the sharpened edge on the box, using the ruler for a guide. If the scissors are sharp, he or she won't need to use much pressure.

2. Neatly cut off the top of the box.

3. Make a cut that starts at the top left corner and stops at the score line. Make another cut from the top right corner to the score line.

4. Bend the front side of the box inward at the score line. Use a strip of masking tape to secure it to the bottom of the box.

5. Cut a piece of heavyweight cardboard that measures 4½ by 9 inches. Glue the cardboard to the back inside of the box. This will strengthen the back of the box to support the weight of 22 CDs.

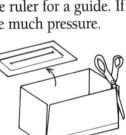

6. Line the inside of the box with black felt. Cut the four pieces needed to fit the inside back, two sides, and bottom, then glue them on. When you cut the piece for the bottom, be sure to cut a piece big enough to wrap around and under the front edge. (See illustration.)

7. Cut pieces of pink felt to fit the outside back and two sides and glue them on.

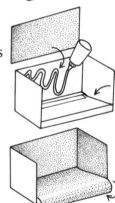

8. Cut a few musical notes out of black felt and glue them onto the outside sides of the box. Now, wasn't that EZ?

Lucky Ladybugs

It is said that if a ladybug lands on you, you will have good luck. Make a bunch of these lucky ladybug pins to put on backpacks, purses, hats, and more.

What You'll Need

- empty pill bottle
- foam sheets or felt, red and black
- pen
- scissors
- tacky craft glue
- black permanent marker
- hole punch
- tiny googly eyes (5 mm size)
- craft pin backings, no bigger than 1 inch long
- black thread

Directions

1. Find an empty pill bottle (with a circular bottom) and place it bottom-end down on the red foam sheet (or felt). The pill bottle is going to be your template. Use a pen and trace around the bottom of the pill bottle onto the foam sheet. Cut out the marked circle and set it aside. This is the body.

2. Cut a small half circle from the black foam sheet (or felt). This will be the head. Using a strong tacky glue, stick the head onto the body as shown.

3. Use the black permanent marker to make a line down the center of the body.

4. Use the hole punch on the black foam sheet (or felt) to make the ladybug spots. Glue the spots onto the body.

5. Glue on two tiny googly eyes. Allow the glue to dry. While you're waiting, make more ladybugs.

6. Once the glue is dry, turn the ladybug over and glue on a craft pin backing. To make antennae, cut a short length of black thread. Pinch the thread at the center and glue it onto the back of the head. Allow the glue to dry. Give some of these ladybug pins to your friends for good fortune.

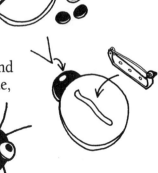

31

Lace-Up Dress-Up

Add some fun to those tired ol' tennies with these colorful charms that stick to your shoelaces.

What You'll Need

- scissors
- foam sheets or felt, various colors
- Velcro
- tacky craft glue
- glitter paint in tubes with a writer's tip, various colors
- rhinestones or sequins (optional)
- pair of tired ol' tennies

Directions

1. Cut out little shapes from the foam sheets (or felt). You can cut out stars, hearts, lightning bolts, rainbows, flowers, geometric shapes, or whatever shapes you can think of. Just try to keep the shapes no bigger than ½ to ¾ inch long in any one direction. Be sure to use a variety of colors.

2. Separate the Velcro pieces. For this craft, you're going to use only the rough piece of Velcro, the side with the tiny loops on it. (You will not need the smooth, soft piece.) Cut tiny pieces of rough Velcro to fit each shape. Use a tacky craft glue to glue the Velcro to the back of each shape. Allow the glue to dry.

3. Decorate the top side of each shape with glitter paint, or you can glue on rhinestones or sequins to embellish.

4. Once the paint and glue are dry, simply stick the shapes onto your shoelaces. Show a friend how to make these shoelace charms, then you can mix 'n' match and trade with each other.

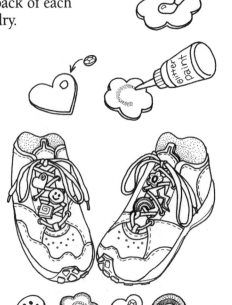

It's About Time

Get together with your best friend to make this time capsule full of "timely" mementos from your friendship.

What You'll Need

- scissors
- construction paper, various colors
- potato chip can with lid (such as Pringles)
- glue
- fine-tip markers
- mementos (see Step 5 for suggestions)

Directions

1. Invite your best friend over to help you make this craft. Cut a piece of construction paper to fit around the potato chip can. (You can also use a coffee can or oatmeal box.) Glue the construction paper onto the can.

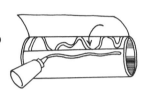

2. On the can, use markers to write the words "Time Capsule," both your names, and today's date. If you want, you can use a futuristic letter style like the one shown here. All the lettering should take up about half the space on the can.

3. Decorate the other half of the can with clock graphics. To make these graphics, cut out three 1½-inch-size circles or ovals from white or a light-colored construction paper. These will be the clock faces. With the fine-tip marker, draw on the numbers and hands of the clock.

4. Cut three more circles or ovals out of bright-colored construction paper that are a little bigger than the clock faces. Glue the clock faces onto the larger pieces. Glue the clocks onto the can.

5. Now comes the fun part. You and your friend need to gather stuff to put in the time capsule. Photos are a must, but you can also include notes to one another or anything that may hold a special memory of your friendship. Get out some old teen magazines and cut out pictures of your favorite rock stars. Cut out pictures of stylish clothes and hairdos. Clip articles about important events from magazines or newspapers. Put all these things into the time capsule and put on the lid. Now hide the time capsule in a place where you can forget about it. Years from now, when you rediscover it, you'll be reminded of a wonderful, timeless friendship.

Three-Level Lava Lamp

This is one way-cool decorative item. Make one for your most way-cool buddy.

What You'll Need

- two empty plastic peanut butter jars with lids, one 8-ounce size and one 12-ounce size
- duct tape
- mini-flashlight, about 2½ inches long
- light corn syrup
- two plastic cups, 8-ounce size
- red and blue food coloring
- two spoons
- water
- corn oil

Directions

1. Remove any labeling from the peanut butter jars and make sure they are clean. Remove the lids and place the jars bottom to bottom. Start wrapping the duct tape around the jars where they meet. Continue wrapping the duct tape downward until it covers the smaller jar to the lid threads.

2. Use duct tape to secure the bottom end of the flashlight to the inside of the smaller jar's lid. Screw the lid onto the smaller jar.

3. Set the jars down with the open jar facing up. Pour light corn syrup into a plastic cup until it is about 1½ inches from the top of the cup. Add two or three drops of red food coloring to the syrup and mix completely with a spoon. Pour the red corn syrup into the jar.

4. Pour water into the other plastic cup until it is about 1½ inches from the top. Add one or two drops of blue food coloring and mix well with a clean spoon. Pour the blue water into the jar.

5. Fill the rest of the jar, just shy of the top, with corn oil. Put the lid on tightly.

6. Unscrew the bottom lid, turn on the light, and replace the lid. Gently shake the lava lamp to mix up the colors. Now sit back and watch the colors move as they slowly settle back into place.

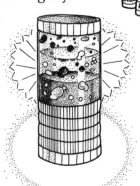

Make Scents

Make this air freshener for a dear friend. It will fill the room with the sweet smell of her favorite perfume.

What You'll Need

- scissors
- foam sheets or felt in purple, yellow, and orange
- tacky craft glue (or hot glue gun with adult supervision)
- hole punch
- ¼-inch-wide purple satin ribbon, 12 inches long
- friend's favorite perfume

Directions

1. Use the illustration shown here as a guide and cut out the flower pattern from a purple foam sheet (or felt).

2. Cut two 1½-inch circles from a yellow foam sheet (or felt).

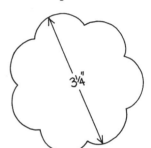

3. Use a strong tacky glue to glue a yellow circle onto the center of the purple flower. Turn the flower over and glue the second yellow circle onto the other side of the flower.

4. Use the hole punch to punch out five small circles from the orange foam sheet (or felt). Glue the five orange circles onto the yellow center of the flower. Turn the flower over and do the same on the other side.

5. Use the hole punch to make a hole at the top of the flower. Bring the two ends of the satin ribbon together and tie them into a knot. Stick the looped end of the ribbon through the hole at the top of the flower. Bring the knotted end of the ribbon through the loop and pull tight.

6. Get ahold of a bottle of your friend's favorite perfume. Spray each side of the flower two or three times. Give the air freshener to your friend just as it is, or use it as an embellishment on a gift. The perfume should last two or three weeks. Once the aroma fades, tell her to simply respray it.

35

Fun and Fuzzy Frame

This boa-trimmed picture frame is the perfect way to display a photo of that special friend.

What You'll Need

- 4-by-6-inch photo of your best friend(s)
- scissors
- poster board, 8½ by 11 inches
- ruler
- pencil
- color pencil (same color as boa)
- glue
- lightweight boa, 24 inches long
- 3-by-5-inch index card

Directions

1. This picture frame is made to fit a standard 4-by-6-inch photo. If your photo is a different size, make measurement adjustments so that your photo will fit. Cut out two pieces of poster board that measure 5½ by 7½ inches.

2. Using the ruler and pencil, lightly mark a 1-inch border around all four sides of one of the pieces of poster board. Cut out the window. (The window should measure 3½ by 5½ inches.)

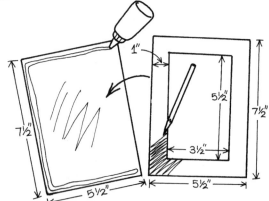

3. Use the color pencil that is the same color as the boa to color in the front of the frame.

4. Squirt a line of glue along the edges of the two shorter sides and one longer side of the plain poster board. Place the poster board with the window cut out on top of the plain one, color side faceup. (The side left unglued will be the side you will later slip your photo into.)

5. Squirt a line of glue around the border of the frame and glue the boa onto it. Cut off any excess boa. Allow the glue to dry before going on to the next step.

6. To make a stand for the frame, take the index card and measure 1¼ inches down from the longer edge. Make a light pencil line.

7. If your photo is vertical, glue the stand onto the back side of the frame along one of the shorter sides. Be sure to line up the bottom edge of the frame with the 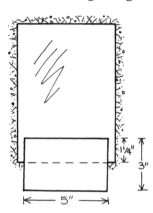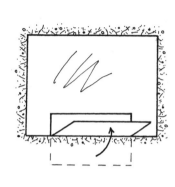 light pencil line on the stand. If your photo is horizontal, glue the stand onto the longer glued (closed) edge of the frame. Again, be sure to line up the bottom edge of the frame with the light pencil line on the stand. With a horizontal picture, make sure the open edge of the frame is at the top. Once the glue is dry, bend the stand upward along the pencil line. The stand should stick up perpendicular to the frame.

8. Slip the photo into the frame through the open edge.

Wind Spinner

ADULT SUPERVISION REQUIRED
Not only is this spinning wind toy fun to watch, it's also fun to make. Create one for a friend.

What You'll Need

- 2-liter plastic soda bottle
- utility knife (to be used only by an adult)
- hole punch
- scissors
- string or yarn
- fisherman's swivel (available at sporting goods stores)
- stickers
- permanent markers, various colors
- three colors of ribbon, each ½ inch wide and 1 yard long
- 18 plastic pony beads, various colors

Directions

1. Rinse out the plastic soda bottle and remove the label. Get an adult to do this next part. Using the illustration shown here as a guide, have an adult cut a C shape into the side of the plastic bottle with the utility knife. The C shape should be approximately 1½ inches wide and 4½ inches long.

2. Have the adult make three more C-shaped cuts (for a total of four), spacing them out evenly around the surface of the bottle.

3. Bend all four C-shaped flaps outward, creasing them so that they stick out perpendicular to the surface of the bottle. These four flaps are the wind catchers.

4. Use the hole punch to make a hole above each window. It will take a little muscle, so if you've tried and can't do it, get an adult to help you.

5. Cut four 12-inch lengths of string or yarn. Tie one end of each string to the hole above each window. Gather up all four strings to meet at the bottom of the bottle and tie them in a tight knot.

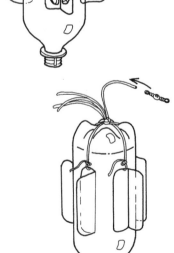

6. Tie on the fisherman's swivel to one of the strings at the bottom of the bottle. Make sure you knot it on tightly. Cut a 24-inch length of string or yarn. Knot one end to the remaining loop of the swivel. Tie a loop for hanging on the other end of the string. Trim all excess string. The fisherman's swivel will freely rotate when the bottle spins, preventing the string from overtwisting.

7. Decorate the outside of the spinner with stickers and permanent markers. Be creative!

8. Gather up all three 1-yard lengths of ribbon and tie them on as shown around the neck of the bottle. Put three plastic pony beads onto each ribbon end. Make double knots at the ends of the ribbons to hold the beads on. You're done! Hang the wind spinner up in a tree or on your patio, where it can catch the wind.

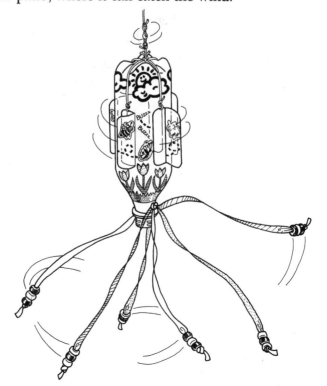

Bookworm

This busy little bookworm is an excellent bookmark. Give one to a friend!

What You'll Need

- scissors
- light green foam sheet or felt, at least 3 by 8 inches
- green permanent marker
- ruler
- light green and black embroidery floss
- embroidery needle with large eye
- five red or orange pom-poms (1½-inch size)
- one red or orange pom-pom (½-inch size)
- hole punch
- yellow foam sheet or felt
- glue
- two tiny googly eyes (5 mm size)

Directions

1. Cut a leaf shape from the light green foam sheet (or felt). Use the green permanent marker to draw veins on the leaf.

2. Thread a 12-inch length of light green embroidery floss onto the needle. Make a triple knot at the end of the floss. Stick the needle through the center of one of the larger-size pom-poms. Pull the floss until the knot stops it. Thread the remaining five pom-poms onto the floss with the smaller pom-pom put on last. The smaller pom-pom is the worm's head. Pull the floss tight and make a double knot.

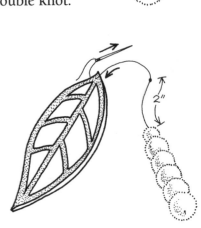

3. The needle and floss should still be attached to the worm. Starting at the worm's head, measure down the floss 2 inches. Make a double knot in the floss at the 2-inch spot. Poke the needle into the top point of the leaf. Continue to pull the floss until the knot meets the leaf's surface. Make a triple knot in the floss on the back side of the leaf. Trim off any excess floss.

4. Use the hole punch to punch out 10 to 12 tiny circles from the yellow foam sheet (or felt). Glue the yellow dots onto the worm's body.

5. Glue on the googly eyes.

6. To make antennae, thread the needle with a 3-inch length of black embroidery floss. Make a triple knot at the end of the floss. Poke the needle into the top of the head as shown and pull until the antennae are the length you like. Put a triple knot in the remaining antenna and trim off any excess floss.

7. Once all the glue is dry, you can use your bookworm bookmark. Place the leaf into the book, and allow the worm to dangle down on the outside cover. Once your friends see it, they'll want you to make them one, too.

Daisy Crazy

Daisies are known as the flower of friendship. This daisy pillow will make a thoughtful gift.

What You'll Need

(The following supplies are enough for two pillows.)
- pinking shears
- ruler
- pink and light green cotton fabric, ½ yard each color
- wire cutters
- two silk daisies, 3 to 3½ inches in diameter
- strong tacky craft glue (or hot glue gun with adult supervision)
- scissors
- sheet of clear acetate, 0.005-inch thickness, at least 7 by 10 inches (available at art supply stores)
- straight pins
- pink and light green embroidery floss
- embroidery needle
- polyester pillow stuffing, 8-ounce bag

Directions

1. Use the pinking shears to cut a 10-inch square from the pink fabric and another from the light green fabric.

2. Next, use the pinking shears to cut a 4½-inch square from the light green fabric.

3. Use wire cutters to trim off the stem of one of the daisies as close to the flower as possible. Use a strong tacky craft glue (or hot glue gun with an adult's help) to glue the daisy onto the center of the 4½-inch square of light green fabric. Allow the glue to dry.

4. Place the square with the daisy on it down flat in the center of the large pink fabric square in a diamond shape, as shown on the next page. Cut a 3¾-inch square of acetate and place it over the daisy. Use a straight pin at the top and bottom points of the acetate diamond to hold everything in place. Be sure that the straight pins go through all three layers of the material (the acetate, the light green fabric, and the pink fabric).

5. Cut a 24-inch length of pink embroidery floss. Embroidery floss contains six threads twisted together. Separate the six threads into two sets of three and pull them apart. Thread one of the lengths of floss onto the embroidery needle. Put a knot in the end. Starting from

the back side, stitch the acetate window and daisy diamond onto the pink fabric square. The stitch used is a simple straight stitch, going in and out as you make your way around. Be sure to stay at least ¼ inch away from the edge of the acetate as you stitch. When you're done, be sure to knot and trim the floss on the back side of the fabric. Remove the two straight pins.

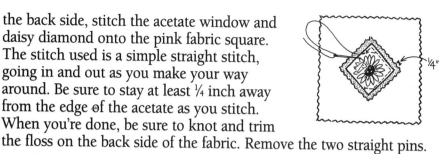

6. Place the pink square (with the daisy now attached) on top of the 10-inch light green square, wrong sides together. Be sure to match up all the edges. Use about eight straight pins to hold the squares together.

7. Cut a 24-inch length of light green embroidery floss. Separate the floss into two sets of three threads. Thread one of the lengths onto the embroidery needle. Put a knot in the end of the floss. Using the same simple stitch, sew the two squares together, staying about ½ inch from the edge of the fabric. If you run out of floss, make a knot and continue with another length of floss. When you're done sewing three sides together, stop and knot the floss.

8. Stuff the pillow through the unsewn side with polyester stuffing. Once you have enough stuffing inside, sew the fourth side closed. Knot and trim the floss on the back side of the pillow. You're done! You should have enough materials to make another pillow, so you can give one to a friend and keep one for yourself.

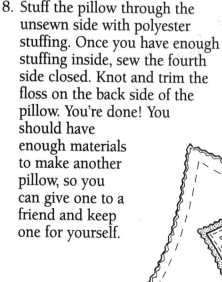

Animal Magnetism

Are you and your best friend great animal lovers? If so, then get together and make these fun decorator magnets.

What You'll Need

- photos of your pets or clippings from old magazines
- scissors
- magnetic strip, at least 2 inches wide (available at most craft stores)
- glue

Directions

1. Do you own a dog, cat, bird, fish, horse, turtle, iguana, rabbit, guinea pig, or some other critter? Gather up photos of your pet(s), and check with an adult to see if it would be all right to cut up these photos. If it's OK, neatly cut out the animal(s). Stay as close as possible to the animal's body as you cut out each one. If you can't cut up the photos or if you don't have a pet of your own, look through old magazines and neatly cut out pictures of any animals that you like. The animals can be wild or domestic, but be sure they're no bigger than 2 inches in any one direction. You can even cut out words such as "dog," "cat," "meow," or "horse."

2. Lay out the magnetic strip flat on a work surface. Glue the photo or magazine cutouts onto the magnetic strip. Allow the glue to completely dry.

3. Using scissors, neatly and carefully cut the magnetic strip around each animal. That's it. Your refrigerator will look like the wild kingdom! You can also cut out pictures of you and your friend, or other subjects from magazines, such as flowers, jewelry, or lips, and make decorator magnets out of them all.

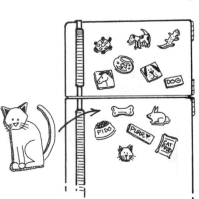

Rock Candy

ADULT SUPERVISION REQUIRED
Here's an old-fashioned treat that you can make with your friends. But you'll have to be patient. Rock candy can take up to three weeks to form.

What You'll Need

- 1 cup water
- saucepan
- stove
- 2 cups sugar
- small bowl
- soup spoon
- wooden spoon
- food coloring (optional)
- six to eight baby food jars
- six to eight Popsicle sticks

Directions

1. You will need an adult to supervise you and your friends as you make the candy. Pour the water into the saucepan. Place the pan on the stove over low heat. Pour the sugar into the small bowl.

2. Add one spoonful of sugar from the bowl to the water and stir with a wooden spoon until the sugar dissolves. Continue adding spoonfuls of sugar and stirring.

3. Continue to stir the solution with the wooden spoon. (A wooden spoon will not get hot like a metal one will.) Once the water starts to get hot, the sugar will dissolve more quickly. Continue adding the sugar spoonful by spoonful. Be sure to stir constantly.

4. Once all the sugar is added, bring the solution to a boil. Boil for about a minute while stirring. The solution should be thick and clear and all sugar crystals should be dissolved. Turn off the heat.

5. If you want to add a few drops of food coloring, now is the time to do it. Stir the solution until it is an even color.

6. Have an adult pour the hot solution evenly into six to eight baby food jars. Place a Popsicle stick into each jar of solution. Place the jars in a spot where they won't be disturbed. The candy will start to crystallize around the Popsicle sticks as the water slowly evaporates. Check the jars every few days. If a crusty layer has formed on the surface, gently break it up with another Popsicle stick so that the water can continue to evaporate. After about three weeks, you and your friends can enjoy this good old-fashioned treat.

Gone Shopping

ADULT SUPERVISION REQUIRED

Going to the mall with your friends is fun, and it is even better if you have a few dollars to spend. Save up your chore money in this cute bank, and never be caught at the mall with an empty wallet again.

What You'll Need

- 13-ounce coffee can with lid
- foam sheets, colors of your choice plus a skin-colored sheet
- hot glue gun (with adult supervision) or tacky craft glue and masking tape
- paper
- pencil
- ruler
- scissors
- poster board
- fine-tip permanent markers, red and black
- utility knife (only to be used by an adult)
- lace, buttons, bows, charms, and rhinestones
- ribbon (optional)
- rouge and eye shadow (optional)

Directions

1. Clean the coffee can by rinsing it in warm water. Dry it completely. Make sure the lid is on the can before you continue.

2. Wrap the can with a foam sheet in the color of your choice. Glue the foam sheet onto the can. A hot glue gun works best for this craft, but use it only with adult supervision. (If you use tacky glue, place a few pieces of masking tape on the spot where the two edges of the foam sheet meet. This will hold it in place while the glue dries. As you glue on the pieces with tacky glue throughout this project, use masking tape where needed to hold the pieces in place. Once the glue is dry, remove the tape.)

3. On a piece of paper, draw a face that looks like yours. Use the illustration shown here as a guide. The entire head should be approximately 3 inches tall and no more than 3 inches wide at the bottom. Again, look at the illustration and draw a base piece that is about 1 inch deep, as shown. Cut out the head (with base attached).

4. Place the head cutout on a piece of poster board and trace around it. Cut it out.

5. Cut the base off your original drawing and place the head flat on the piece of skin-colored foam sheet. Use the pencil to trace around the head. Cut it out. Glue the skin-colored head onto the poster board head.

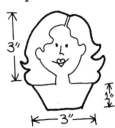

6. Cut the hair off your original drawing. Lay the hair down flat on a foam sheet in a color that matches your own hair. Trace around the hair and cut it out. Glue the hair on top of the head.

7. Use the red fine-tip permanent marker to draw on heart-shaped lips. Use the black fine-tip permanent marker to draw in the eyes and nose.

8. Bend the base piece of the head back and glue it onto the lid of the can as shown.

9. It's time to make the arms. Use the sample shown here as a guide. Cut the arms out of the foam sheet in the color of your choice. Cut out two hands from the skin-colored foam sheet and glue them onto the arms. Glue the arms onto the sides of the can at the shoulders. Bend each arm to the front of the body and glue down the hands.

10. Two poster board rectangles will be shopping bags. One rectangle can be 2 inches wide and 2½ inches tall. The second can be a little smaller. Use the black marker to write your name on the smaller bag. Write "Mall Money" on the larger bag. Glue the two bags onto the front of the body just below the hands. Use the black marker to draw the bag handles.

11. Have an adult use the utility knife to cut a slit in the lid of the can just behind the head.

12. Now comes the fun! Glue on lace, buttons, bows, charms . . . anything you like to dress up your lady shopper. Just be sure you don't glue down something that would keep the lid from being removed. Glue on rhinestones for earrings. You can even make her a little purse cut from a foam sheet with a ribbon for a handle and glue it onto her shoulder. Finally, you may want to apply a little rouge and eye shadow. Now, let's go shopping!

47

Sweet Dreams

Next time you host a slumber party, have each of your guests make one of these overnight bags. They make a terrific party favor for each girl to take home.

- scissors
- ruler
- dark blue or purple standard-size pillowcase (the kind with a hem at the open end)
- masking tape
- 3/16- to 1/4-inch cotton cording, 48 inches long
- large safety pin

- two pieces of yellow felt, 9 by 12 inches
- poster board, 18 by 24 inches
- dark blue or purple embroidery floss (to match the pillowcase)
- embroidery needle
- crystal glitter paint (in a bottle with a fine-line writing tip)

Directions

1. Cut a small 1/2-inch-long slit in the hemmed edge of the pillowcase just to one side of the side seam. It is important that the slit be no more than 1/2 inch long, so do it carefully.

2. Wrap a piece of masking tape around each end of the cotton cording to keep it from unraveling. Slip a large safety pin onto one end of the cording just below the masking tape. Push the safety pin into the slit of the pillowcase. Gather and pull the safety pin through the hem until it reaches the slit again. Pull the safety pin out through the slit. Remove the safety pin and tie the two ends of the cord together in a knot. Remove the masking tape.

3. It's time to decorate the bag. Cut a large crescent moon shape from the yellow felt. The moon should be at least 9 inches tall. Cut five or six stars of different sizes from the yellow felt. The stars should be between 1 and 3 inches tall.

4. Slip a piece of poster board into the pillowcase.

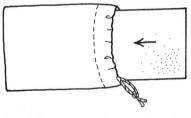

5. Cut a 24-inch length of embroidery floss. Embroidery floss is made up of six threads. Separate the floss into two sets containing three threads apiece. Thread one length of floss onto the embroidery needle and tie a knot in the end.

6. Place the yellow moon on the lower left side of the pillowcase. Tilt the moon at a slight upward angle. Follow the illustration shown here and sew the moon onto the pillowcase with a loop stitch. 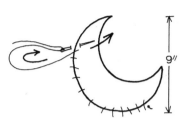 Don't worry about being neat with the stitches. Uneven or crooked stitches will add charm. When you've stitched your way around the entire moon, knot the floss and cut off the excess.

7. Scatter the stars around the moon, and sew them on with a loop stitch. Leave space to the right of the moon for the writing in Step 9.

8. Add some "stardust" by squirting a little crystal glitter paint on the stars. Dab your finger on the stars to spread the glitter evenly. Don't overdo it. A little stardust will go a long way.

9. Using the crystal glitter paint, write "Sweet Dreams" and then your name just to the right of the moon. Allow the bag to dry overnight. In the morning, remove the poster board and the bag will be ready for use.

Tea Party

Invite the girls over for a tea party and serve these fun and tasty cakes.

What You'll Need

- unwrapped cupcakes (enough for one for each girl, plus two more to make the teapot)
- butter knife
- white and chocolate frosting
- small dessert-size paper plates
- small doilies to fit the plates
- candy cane
- Life Savers
- gumdrop
- red shoestring licorice
- M&M's Minis
- milk, punch, or tea

Directions

1. You'll use two cupcakes to make the teapot first. Using a butter knife, put a small dab of white frosting in the center of a small dessert-size paper plate. Press a doily onto the plate. Put a small dab of frosting in the center of the doily. Press one cupcake down onto the doily. Stick the second cupcake onto the first, top to top, with a dab of frosting. Frost the entire outside of the teapot with white frosting.

2. Break off the straight end of the candy cane and stick it into the teapot for a spout. Use the curved end of the candy cane for a handle.

3. To create a lid, place a Life Saver on top of the teapot. Put a small dab of frosting in the center of the Life Saver and press the gumdrop into it.

4. Decorate the rest of the teapot with shoestring licorice and M&M's Minis. You can use the finished illustration as a guide, or do your own thing.

5. Now it's time to make a teacup. Frost only the sides of the teacup with white frosting.

6. Frost the top of the teacup with chocolate frosting.

7. Stick a Life Saver into the side of the teacup for a handle. Decorate the rest of the cup with shoestring licorice and M&M's Minis. You're done! But remember, you have to make a teacup for each girl. Serve your cakes with milk, a favorite punch, or even tea!

Lollipop Garden

Sweet lollipop flowers make a special treat for a friend, or display a bouquet of them in a clay pot as a party centerpiece.

What You'll Need

- scissors
- construction paper, variety of colors
- ruler
- lollipops
- double-faced tape (or regular clear tape)

- green satin ribbon, ¼ inch wide
- 4- to 6-inch clay pot (optional)
- 4- to 6-inch block Styrofoam (optional)
- green tissue paper (optional)

Directions

1. Using the illustrations shown here as a guide, cut flower shapes from the construction paper. You can make a tulip, a daisy, or a rounded-petal-type flower. Whatever flower shape you decide to make, just be sure it's about 3 inches in diameter.

2. Use scissors to neatly trim off the excess wrapping around each lollipop.

3. Put a piece of double-faced tape down on the center of the flower cutout. (If you don't have double-faced tape, you can use a loop of regular clear tape.) Place the lollipop down onto the center of the flower.

4. To make the leaves, cut a 10-inch length of green satin ribbon. Tie it onto the lollipop stick in a bow. That's it! Assemble the remaining flowers.

5. If you want to make a centerpiece display, here's how: Have an adult help you trim a Styrofoam block so that it fits snugly inside a clay pot. Now simply push the lollipop sticks into the Styrofoam. Shred up some green tissue paper to put into the pot to hide the Styrofoam. Your lollipop garden is ready for pickin' and lickin'.

Butterfly Twist

This twisting mobile of fluttering butterflies is the perfect decorative item for a friend's room. Make one for yourself, too.

What You'll Need

- scissors
- ruler
- colored poster board, at least 12 by 12 inches
- six pieces of card stock (color of your choice, at least 3 by 5 inches)
- paper
- pencil
- black fine-tip marker
- hole punch
- white thread
- pushpin
- stapler

Directions

1. Cut a 12-inch circle out of the colored poster board. Starting at the edge of the circle, cut a spiral toward the center. (See the dotted line in the illustration shown here.) The spiral should make at least three rotations and end in a circle at the center as shown.

2. Look carefully at the illustration, and cut away the areas indicated by shading. Set the spiral aside.

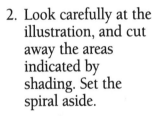

3. You are now ready to make the butterflies. The butterflies will be made from card stock. First, use the illustration shown here as a guide to make a butterfly template out of paper or scrap poster board.

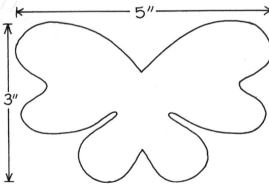

4. Using your template and the pencil, trace five or six butterflies onto different colors of card stock. Cut out the butterflies.

5. Use the marker to draw a few details on the butterflies' wings. Since both sides of each wing will be seen, you'll have to turn over the butterfly and draw the design on the other side, too.

6. Use the hole punch to make a hole in the outer end of the spiral. Tie a length of thread onto the hole. Hang the spiral from the ceiling using the pushpin, but hang it low enough for you to reach all parts of it.

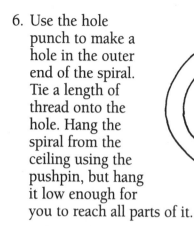

7. Staple each butterfly down its center onto the spiral. Space them out evenly and fold up each butterfly's wings. Rehang the spiral at the height you want and you're done. As air moves through the room, the butterflies will spin around.

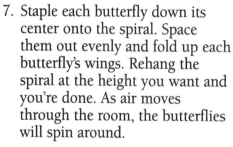

Staple

Push-Up Party Popper

These party poppers will add great fun to your next bash.

What You'll Need

- toilet paper rolls (one for each guest)
- plastic pushers from push-up ice creams (one for each guest)
- wrapping paper
- pencil
- ruler
- scissors
- clear tape
- colorful tissue and scrap paper
- metallic confetti (optional)
- masking tape

Directions

1. First, you've got to save toilet paper rolls and then you've got to eat a lot of push-up ice creams and save the plastic pusher parts. Wash the pushers with a little soap and water, then rinse. Allow them to dry completely. Once you have saved up enough rolls and pushers for a party, you can make the party poppers. Follow Steps 2 through 8, then repeat for as many poppers as you need.

2. Place a toilet paper roll down on one end on the wrong side of a piece of wrapping paper. Use the pencil to trace around the base of the roll. Remove the roll and with the aid of a ruler, add ¾ inch around the entire circle, marking it with a pencil. Cut out the larger circle.

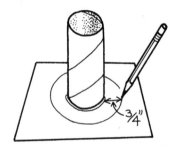

3. Fold the circle in half with the wrong side of the wrapping paper on the outside. Cut a slit in the center of the circle starting at the folded edge and stopping just shy of the pencil line. Unfold the circle. Refold the circle in the opposite direction and cut another slit. Unfold the circle. You should end up with an X-shaped slit inside the circle.

4. Cut the toilet paper roll in half and discard the top.

5. Center the wrapping paper circle, right side faceup, on top of the end of the roll. (Be gentle, since you don't want any of the slits to tear.) Bring the overhanging part of the circle down onto the side of the roll and secure it with tape.

6. Cut a piece of wrapping paper to fit the outside of the roll. Tape one edge of the paper to the roll as shown and wrap the paper around the roll, then secure it with tape.

7. Make confetti by cutting up pieces of colorful tissue and scrap paper. Fill the upside-down popper about three-quarters of the way with confetti. You can buy some metallic confetti at a party store and include that, too.

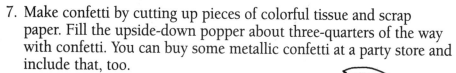

8. Test to see if the pusher fits snugly inside the popper. If it is too loose, wrap the outside rim of the pusher with layers of masking tape. Insert the plastic pusher into the open end of the popper, but only push it in about ½ inch.

9. To work the popper, all you have to do is quickly push the stick up into the tube. The slits in the top will split apart, allowing the confetti to fly. Now, that's a party-poppin' good time!

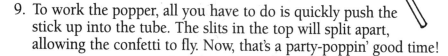

35 Bless You!

Next time your friend asks you for a tissue, hand her one from your stylish tissue holder. If she likes it, make one for her, too.

What You'll Need

- scissors
- felt, various colors
- ruler
- four straight pins
- embroidery floss, any color
- embroidery needle
- tacky craft glue
- pocket pack of tissues (the kind that fits in a purse)

Directions

1. Cut a piece of felt to measure 6½ by 5½ inches. Lay the felt flat in a rectangle as shown. Bring the left and right sides in to meet at the middle. Use the straight pins (two on the top and two on the bottom) to hold the sides down.

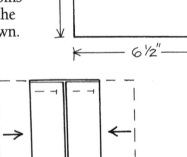

2. Thread a needle with a 16-inch length of embroidery floss. Tie a knot in the end. Start at the lower right corner of the felt. From the back side, poke the needle up through the felt and pull the floss until the knot stops it.

3. Now poke the needle back down into the front side of the felt, and start pulling the floss. Stop pulling when you see the floss form a loop. Poke the needle up through the loop and pull the floss tight. Poke the needle back down into the front side of the felt just to the

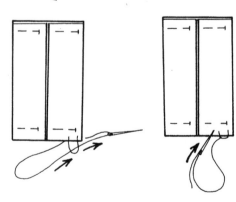

left of the first stitch and repeat this step. This is called a blanket stitch. Stitch the entire bottom edge closed with a blanket stitch. When you reach the end, make a knot and trim the excess floss.

4. Sew the top edge closed with a blanket stitch. Remove the straight pins.

5. Cut out flowers, butterflies, or whatever shapes you want from different colors of felt. Use a strong tacky craft glue to adhere the decorations onto the tissue holder.

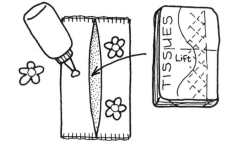

6. Open the slit of the tissue holder and insert the pocket pack of tissues. You're done!

Make a Switch Plate

This colorful light switch plate is a fun decorative item for your (or a friend's) room.

What You'll Need

- two paintbrushes, one medium and one fine-tip
- wooden light switch plate
- acrylic paints in a "rainbow" of colors plus sky (light) blue
- scissors
- white foam sheet or felt
- glue

Directions

1. Using a medium-size paintbrush, paint the entire light switch plate sky blue. Don't forget to paint all the edges, too. Allow the paint to dry.

2. Using the illustration shown here as a guide, and a fine-tip brush, paint a rainbow. Use a minimum of three different colors—four or five colors look best. Allow the paint to dry.

3. Cut out two cloud shapes from the white foam sheet (or felt). Glue them onto the switch plate as shown. Make sure the screw hole is not covered. It's fine if the clouds extend beyond the edges of the plate. Allow the glue to dry.

4. Install your switch plate. Dab a little paint (in the matching color) onto the heads of the screws.

Petite Pocket Purse

This little purse, made from a jean pocket, is so adorable. This is the perfect craft for you and a friend to do together, since most jeans have two back pockets.

What You'll Need

- pair of old blue jeans (the kind with back pockets)
- pinking shears
- ruler
- blue thread
- needle

Directions

1. First, get permission to cut up a pair of old jeans. Once you've gotten the OK, use pinking shears to cut just around the outside edges of the back pocket. Guess what? You're done with the purse, and all you have left to do is make and attach the handle.

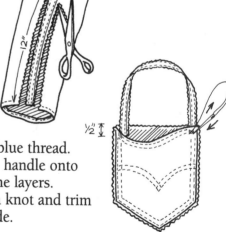

2. To make the handle, simply use pinking shears to cut on either side of the inner pant leg seam. Make the handle 12 inches in length.

3. Slip the two ends of the handle about ½ inch down inside the purse as shown, and close the purse flat.

4. Thread a needle with a piece of blue thread. Make a knot in the end. Sew the handle onto the purse by going through all the layers. Make three or four stitches, then knot and trim the excess thread on the back side.

One Step Further

Embellish your pocket purse with an iron-on appliqué. (Have an adult handle the hot iron.) Take a trip to a fabric or craft store. You should be able to find a wide variety of iron-on appliqués to choose from, such as butterflies, flowers, rainbows, stars, peace symbols, or just about anything you like!

Fancy Flip-Flops

This summer you and your friends will be fashion trendsetters in these fun and fancy flip-flops.

What You'll Need

- pinking shears
- scrap fabric (cotton calico type works best)
- ruler
- pair of inexpensive flip-flops, a half-size bigger than your regular size

Directions

1. Using pinking shears, cut strips of fabric that measure 1 by 8 inches. You will have to cut around 40 pieces to cover two flip-flops.

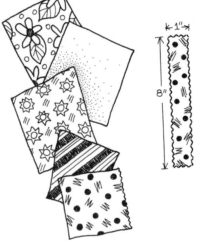

2. Starting on one flip-flop, tie a strip of fabric onto the strap. Tie a tight knot. Continue knotting on the strips of fabric until you have covered the entire strap. Do the same with the other flip-flop. You're now ready for summer fun!

Hang It Up

Tired of your necklaces being in knots? Tired of losing rings? This jewelry hanger will help you and your friends organize your jewelry.

What You'll Need

- ¼-inch dowel, 10 inches long
- acrylic craft paint, any color
- small paintbrush
- needle-nose pliers
- 18-gauge wire, 18 inches long
- ruler
- two small nails
- hammer

Directions

1. Paint the dowel with acrylic paint in the color of your choice. Set the dowel aside to dry, and go on to the next step.

2. The use of needle-nose pliers will make these next few steps easy. Bend the wire in half. Loop the left and right sections of the wire back down, as shown, creating a heart shape. Twist the wires together with one rotation at the spot where they meet.

3. The excess wire should extend out straight from the bottom tip of the heart as shown. Measure 3 inches from the bottom tip of the heart and bend the wires up to be perpendicular.

4. Look at the illustration carefully as a guide. Place the dowel (once it's dry) down about 1 inch from the bend in the wires. With the help of the needle-nose pliers, loop the remaining wire up and over the dowel.

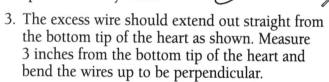

5. Place your new jewelry hanger on the wall with two small nails, using the hammer. To hang necklaces and bracelets, undo the clasps and loop them onto the center section of the dowel. For rings, simply slide them onto either end.

Bizzy, Bizzy Bee

This date book will help you keep track of your busy days . . . soccer games, school assignments, cheerleading practice, movie dates with friends, and more.

What You'll Need

- date book
- yellow construction paper
- pencil
- ruler
- scissors
- glue
- yellow, black, and white felt
- black permanent marker
- black thread
- six tiny googly eyes (5 mm size)

Directions

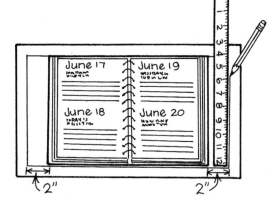

1. You're going to make a book cover first. Open up the date book and lay it down on the sheet of yellow construction paper. Use a pencil to trace around the outside of the book. With a ruler, measure 2 inches past the left side and draw a line. Do the same on the right. Remove the date book and cut out the book cover.

2. Squirt a line of glue all around the outer edges of the book cover. Wrap the book cover around the date book, and wrap the left and right ends around to the inside of the front and back covers.

3. Cut out three small oval bee bodies from the yellow felt. Cut out three small half-circle shapes from the black felt for the heads. Cut out six teardrop shapes from the white felt for the wings.

4. Glue the three yellow bee bodies onto the front cover, making sure to space them out. Glue the black heads onto the bodies.

5. Use the black permanent marker to draw two or three stripes on the bee bodies. Now glue on the wings.

6. Cut tiny lengths of black thread for the antennae and stinger. Use a tiny dot of glue to glue them on. Glue on the googly eyes.

7. Use the black permanent marker to make little dashed lines coming from the stinger end of each bee. You can even write "[your name] is a Bizzy, Bizzy Bee." If your best friend likes your new date book, make one for her, too.

Home "Tweet" Home

ADULT SUPERVISION REQUIRED
This sweet little birdhouse is a fun project to do with a friend.

What You'll Need

- clean 16-ounce cottage cheese container, with lid
- hole punch
- utility knife (to be used only by an adult)
- ruler
- gesso paint (found at art supply stores) or white primer paint
- medium and small paintbrushes
- acrylic paint, various colors
- twig
- garden clippers
- hot glue gun (with adult supervision)
- ⅛- to ³⁄₁₆-inch cotton cord, 18 inches long

Directions

1. Take the lid off the cottage cheese container. Use the hole punch to make a hole in the side of the container as shown.

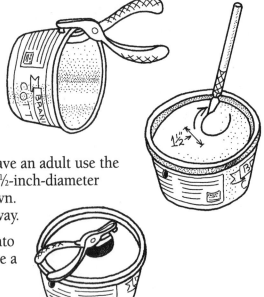

2. Put the lid back onto the container. Have an adult use the utility knife to cut a 1½-inch-diameter hole in the lid as shown. This hole is the doorway.

3. Slip the hole punch into the doorway and make a hole just below it.

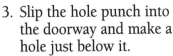

4. Before you start painting, make sure the doorway is lined up with the hole at the top of the birdhouse. If it isn't, readjust the lid now. Paint the entire birdhouse with white gesso (or primer) paint. Allow the paint to dry, then paint on a second layer. Allow the second layer to dry.

5. Use acrylic paints to paint your birdhouse any way you like. Allow the paint to dry.

6. Go hunting for a small twig that will fit snugly into the hole under the doorway. Use clippers to trim the twig to be 4 inches long. Insert the twig about 1 inch into the hole. Ask an adult to help you use the hot glue gun on the part of the twig that is inside the birdhouse to seal it. Allow the glue to cool off.

7. Stick one end of the cotton cord into the hole at the top and pull that end out through the doorway. Tie a knot in the end of the cord. Pull the cord from the top of the birdhouse until the knot stops it. Tie a loop in the other end of the cord to be used for hanging. Hang the birdhouse in your yard or garden. Some lucky bird will make it her home "tweet" home.

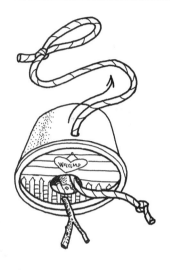

Candy-Keeper Key Chain

ADULT SUPERVISION REQUIRED

Everybody is going to want one of these key chains full of sweets. Make one for each of your friends.

What You'll Need

- clear plastic dome container with cap (the kind you get out of a gumball machine with a prize inside) or empty clear plastic pill bottle with cap
- thick magazine

- hammer
- large nail
- scissors
- cotton string
- assorted small candies
- key ring, 1 inch in diameter

Directions

1. Remove the cap from the container or pill bottle. (If you are using a pill bottle, be sure to first wash it out well and remove the label.) Place the cap upside down on a thick magazine. Have an adult help you use the hammer and large nail to make a hole in the center of the cap.

2. Cut a 12-inch length of cotton string. Fold it in half and insert the two ends into the hole on the top side of the cap. Continue pulling the string until the loop coming out of the top is about 2 inches in length. Tie the string into a knot on the inside of the cap. Trim off any excess string.

3. Fill the container (or pill bottle) with assorted small candies. Place the cap back onto the container.

4. Place the "candy keeper" onto a key ring and you're done!

One Step Further

Use puff paints—in bottles with fine writing tips—to personalize and decorate the candy keeper. Write your friend's name on the outside. Decorate the top and sides with simple designs such as polka dots, stripes, stars, or flowers.

43 Purple Cow

Next time a group of friends comes over, serve up this cool and smooth dairy treat. This recipe serves four.

What You'll Need

- 3 cups vanilla nonfat frozen yogurt
- 1 cup reduced fat milk
- ½ cup thawed frozen grape juice concentrate (undiluted)
- 1½ teaspoons lemon juice
- blender
- four glasses
- four straws

Directions

1. Put the frozen yogurt, milk, grape juice concentrate, and lemon juice in a blender.

2. Mix the ingredients at medium speed until smooth.

3. Pour into glasses and serve immediately. Don't forget the straws!

Paper Lantern

This is the perfect decorative item for that special friend's room.

What You'll Need

- glue
- 24 Popsicle sticks
- wire cutters
- 18-gauge wire
- ruler
- scissors
- tissue paper, light green, pink, purple, and yellow
- yellow construction paper
- white thread

Directions

1. Glue four Popsicle sticks end to end into a square. Glue four more Popsicle sticks on top of the existing four. Glue the fatter side of a Popsicle stick onto each of the four sides of the square.

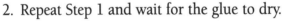

2. Repeat Step 1 and wait for the glue to dry.

3. Use wire cutters to cut four 9-inch pieces of 18-gauge wire. Wrap one end of each wire around each corner of one of the Popsicle squares.

4. Wrap the other four wire ends around the four corners of the other Popsicle square, forming a "box" frame.

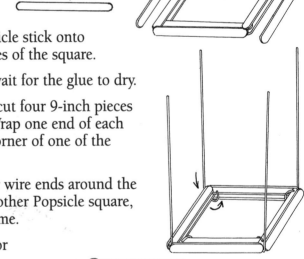

5. To make a hanger for the lantern, cut one more 9-inch length of wire. Bend the wire in half. Bend the ends back up and out to either side, leaving a "bump" in the wire as shown. Lay the hanger across the center top of the lantern frame. Bend the ends of the hanger around the frame as shown.

6. Cut a piece of light green tissue paper to measure 9 by 20 inches and lay it flat on your work surface.

7. Put a thin line of glue on the outside of the vertical Popsicle sticks, top and bottom. Spread out the glue with your pinkie finger. (Using too much glue will ruin the tissue paper.) Place one side of the lantern frame down flat onto the left edge of the tissue paper. Slowly roll the lantern to the right, wrapping the tissue paper onto the frame as you go.

8. Once the lantern is completely wrapped, trim off any excess tissue paper from the top, bottom, and sides of the lantern.

9. Cut out flower shapes from the pink, purple, and yellow tissue paper. Put a tiny dot of glue on the center of each flower and glue them onto the lantern. (Remember, go easy on the glue.) Cut out circular flower centers from the yellow construction paper and glue them onto the center of each flower. To hang up the lantern, tie a piece of white thread to the bump of the wire hanger. To add a little dimension, bend the petals of each flower inward so that the flowers pop off the surface of the lantern.

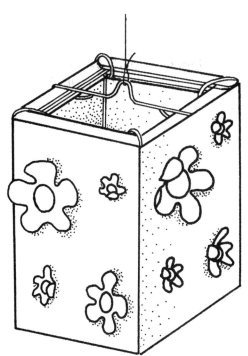

Headbandanna

Here's a quick and easy way to wear a bandanna scarf on your head. Make one for a friend, too.

What You'll Need

(For two headbandannas)
- bandanna
- ruler
- pencil
- scissors
- strong tacky craft glue
- two plastic headbands
- masking tape

Directions

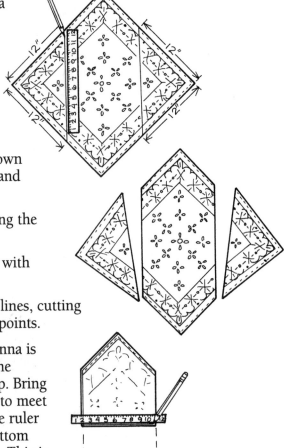

1. Lay the bandanna in a diamond shape on your work surface. Starting at the left point, measure 12 inches up the top left edge and make a pencil mark. From the left point, measure 12 inches down the bottom left edge and make a pencil mark.

2. Make a line connecting the marks.

3. Repeat Steps 1 and 2 with the right point.

4. Cut along the pencil lines, cutting off the left and right points.

5. Make sure the bandanna is now lying flat with the printed side facing up. Bring the bottom point up to meet the top point. Lay the ruler down on the very bottom edge and draw a line. This is the center line.

6. Unfold the bandanna and turn it over so that the wrong side is facing up. Cut the bandanna in half along the center line. You now have two bandanna pieces—one for you, and one for a friend.

7. Squirt a line of glue onto the top side of a plastic headband. Use your finger to spread the glue out evenly across the surface of the headband. Follow the illustration shown here for this next part. Lay the left end of the headband, glue side down, onto the left side of the bandanna (still wrong side up) about 1 inch up from the bottom edge. Put a piece of masking tape across the left end to hold the bandanna in place. Roll the headband to the right and put a piece of masking tape on the right side.

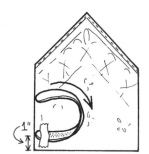

8. Repeat Step 7 with the second headband.

9. Once the glue is dry on both headbands, remove the masking tape. Spread glue onto the bottom section of bandanna just below each headband. Bring the bottom section of bandanna up and over each headband. Use a few pieces of masking tape to hold everything in place. Allow the glue to dry. Remove the masking tape and your headbandannas are ready to wear.

3-D B-D Card

Your friend will love this 3-D pop-up birthday card.

What You'll Need

- scissors
- poster board
- ruler
- foam sheets or construction paper, various colors
- glue
- black fine-tip permanent marker
- markers, various colors
- glitter paint
- pencil

Directions

1. Cut a piece of poster board to measure 8 by 6 inches. Fold the poster board in half, as shown, to create a card.

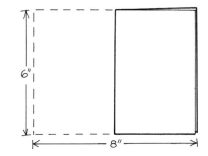

2. Cut three balloon shapes (each one about 2 inches in size) from different color foam sheets (or construction paper) and glue them onto the front of the card. Use the black fine-tip permanent marker to write "For My Friend" on the balloons. Use colorful markers to draw spots of confetti all around the balloons. Draw strings coming from the balloons. Add a few touches of glitter paint and the front of the card is done!

3. Now you'll work on the inside. With a ruler and pencil, lightly draw a rectangle that measures 5 inches wide by 2 inches tall on a piece of poster board. This rectangle will be a birthday cake. Draw a single birthday candle on the center top of the cake. The candle should be about ¾ inch wide and 2 inches high including the flame on top. Cut out the rectangle and candle.

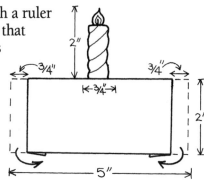

4. Measure ¾ inch from the left and right sides of the cake and make a light line on each side. Fold the two sides to the back side of the cake along the lines as shown. (See illustration for Step 3.)

5. Color and decorate the cake with markers and a little glitter paint. Move on to the next step while the cake dries.

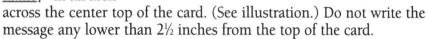

6. Open up the card and use colorful markers to write "Happy Birthday [your friend's name]" in an arch across the center top of the card. (See illustration.) Do not write the message any lower than 2½ inches from the top of the card.

7. Once the cake is dry, turn it over so that the decorated side is facedown. Unfold the two side flaps, then fold the cake (and candle) in half by bringing the right side over to meet the left side.

8. Pick up the folded cake and spread a little glue on the two side flaps. Place the folded cake down on the inside of the opened card ½ inch from the right edge and ¾ inch up from the bottom edge. (See illustration.) Gently close the card. Partially reopen the card after a few minutes to make sure no excess glue has oozed out from behind the cake. If there is any excess glue, wipe it off with your finger and reclose the card to dry.

9. After roughly 10 minutes, the glue should be dry. Open the card. The cake should pop up! You can use markers to write a short message on either side of the cake to complete your 3-D B-D greeting.

You've Got Mail

Store the letters and notes you get from your friends in this custom-made mailbox.

What You'll Need

- one standard-size shoe box, with lid
- ruler
- scissors
- white poster board, at least 22 by 28 inches
- glue
- pencil
- masking tape
- white gesso or primer paint
- medium paintbrush
- red foam sheet (or construction paper)
- hole punch
- white elastic cording
- 1-inch-diameter button (the kind with a loop on the back)
- markers, various colors
- canceled stamps, stickers, and rubber stamps

Directions

1. Remove the lid from the shoe box and set it aside. Measure the long side of the shoe box. Cut a rectangle from the poster board that is the same number of inches high by 22 inches wide.

2. Follow the illustration and bend the poster board rectangle in an arch, then glue it down to the outside of the longer sides of the shoe box. (Since shoe boxes vary in size, you may have to trim a little off the sides of the poster board to get an arch that will best match the arch of a mailbox.) Allow the glue to dry for a few minutes before going on to the next step.

3. Lay the mailbox down on one end, as shown, on top of the poster board. Use a pencil to lightly trace around the mailbox. Cut out the tracing. Lay the cutout you just made down on the remaining poster board, trace it, and cut out a second matching piece.

4. Glue one of the poster board cutouts to the back end of the box. Use masking tape to secure the edges.

5. Now you'll make the door of the mailbox. Cut the four corners of the lid so that it lies completely flat with the right side facing up. Glue the second poster board cutout to the shoe box lid just above the edge crease as shown. Allow the glue a few minutes to dry, then cut around the poster board leaving that little flap attached at the bottom.

6. Cut down the front corners of the box, creating a flap. Glue the door onto the front flap of the mailbox. The bottom flap on the door will be glued to the bottom of the box. Allow the glue to dry.

7. Paint the masking tape at the back edges of the mailbox with white gesso or primer paint.

8. Cut a red flag from the foam sheet (or construction paper). Glue it onto the side of the mailbox.

9. Use the hole punch to make two holes side by side (about ¼ inch apart) near the top edge of the door. Use a piece of white elastic cording to tie a large button onto the door. Knot the elastic on the inside of the door.

10. Use the hole punch to make two holes side by side (about ½ inch apart) in the top arch of the mailbox. Tie a loop of elastic through the holes, knotting it on the inside. The loop should be just the right size to fit securely over the button when the door is closed.

11. Time to decorate! Use colorful markers to write "[your name]: You've Got Mail" on the mailbox, and draw on fun designs and borders. With a parent's permission, cut out canceled stamps from old mail and glue them onto the mailbox. You can also use stickers and rubber stamps to complete the decorations.

Pen Pal

Make this cool pen for that groovy friend!

- lightweight boa, 4 inches long
- masking tape
- nonretractile pen
- white glue
- paper plate
- small paintbrush
- ¾-inch-wide colorful ribbon, 12 inches long
- scissors

Directions

1. Fold the boa in half, matching up the two ends. Use masking tape to tape the two ends of the boa to the top of the pen.

2. Squirt a quarter-size puddle of glue onto the paper plate. Starting at the writing tip of the pen, spread on glue with the brush, but go only halfway up the pen.

3. Hold the ribbon about ½ inch from the end. Place the ribbon onto the writing tip of the pen at a 45-degree angle. (An excess of ½ inch of ribbon will extend beyond the pen tip. You'll trim it later.)

4. Now spin the pen one rotation. Stop and place a small piece of masking tape over the ribbon at the writing tip. The tape will keep the ribbon in place while you are wrapping the ribbon around the pen.

5. Spin the pen, remembering to hold the ribbon at a 45-degree angle as you wrap the pen with the ribbon. Stop when you get halfway up the pen. Apply glue to the upper half of the pen and continue spinning. When you reach the top, stop. Make sure the masking tape at the top is completely covered with ribbon. Place a piece of masking tape on the ribbon at the top to hold it in place while it dries. Clean the brush with warm, soapy water and rinse it well.

6. Wait a few hours for the glue to completely dry, then remove the tape and use scissors to trim the excess ribbon at both the top and writing tip of the pen. Way cool!

Picture This!

Display your favorite photos of you and your friends on this fun photo stand.

What You'll Need

- medium and small paintbrushes
- 2-inch block of wood (available at most craft stores)
- acrylic craft paint, various colors
- needle-nose pliers
- three pieces of 18-gauge wire, each 18 inches long
- wire cutters
- ruler
- hammer
- 18-gauge nail
- white glue
- photos

Directions

1. Use the medium paintbrush to paint the block of wood the desired color. Allow it to dry. Use the small paintbrush to add decorative details such as dainty flowers, polka dots, stripes, stars, hearts, or whatever you come up with. Set the block aside to dry.

2. Use the needle-nose pliers to bend one end of a wire into a spiral-shaped design. You can make a variety of shapes, just as long as the shape spirals around two complete rotations. (See illustrations.) Make a total of three.

3. The straight portions of the wires need to be trimmed with the wire cutters. Measure 6 inches down from the top of one spiral and cut off the excess. Cut the remaining two to measure 5 inches tall.

4. Use the hammer and nail to make three evenly spaced holes in the top of the wood block.

5. Put a tiny spot of glue on top of each nail hole. Push the taller wire into the center hole. Push the two shorter wires into the remaining holes. The glue will ooze out around the base of the wire, but it will dry clear.

6. Once the glue is dry, place your photos in the spiral holders. You can gently bend the wires to flare out the photos.

79

50

Sock It to Me!

These cool and crazy socks will be a big hit with all the girls. They make a fun and inexpensive gift, too.

What You'll Need

- embroidery floss, various colors
- embroidery needle
- assorted buttons, bows, charms, and beads
- pair of bobby socks in white or a color of your choice
- scissors

Directions

1. Thread the embroidery floss on the needle and sew a variety of buttons, bows, charms, and beads onto the cuff edge of a bobby sock. To keep things looking neat, make sure to do all your knotting on the underside of the cuff.

2. For variation, string four or five tiny glass beads onto the embroidery floss. Tie a double knot right under the last bead. Trim the floss about ¼ inch below the knot and fray the threads to create a tassel. You could do the entire cuff this way. The result is one very impressive pair of bobby socks!

3. Tell your friend to wash the decorated socks by hand only and to lay the socks flat on a towel to air dry.

One Step Further

You can make socks with a theme: Christmas, Hanukkah, springtime, western, Halloween, beach lover, animal lover, music lover . . . it's endless! Just pick out the appropriate colored socks, beads, and charms to go with the theme.

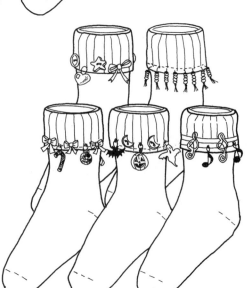